Let's go to Mass

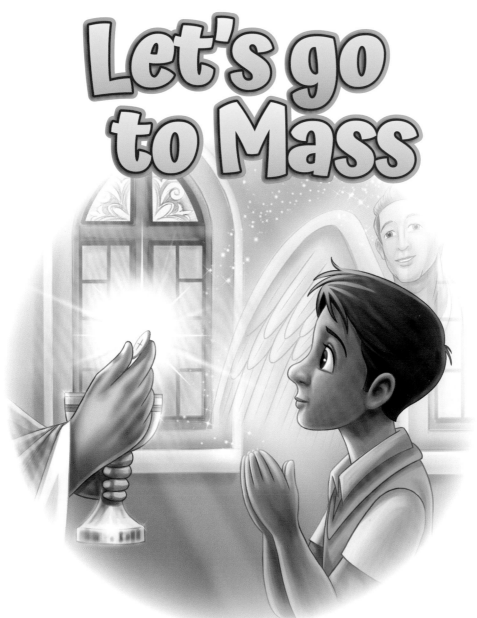

A visual presentation of the Holy Mass

Time to clean up! We are going to visit someone very important!
There is God's house. It's nice and very beautiful!

3

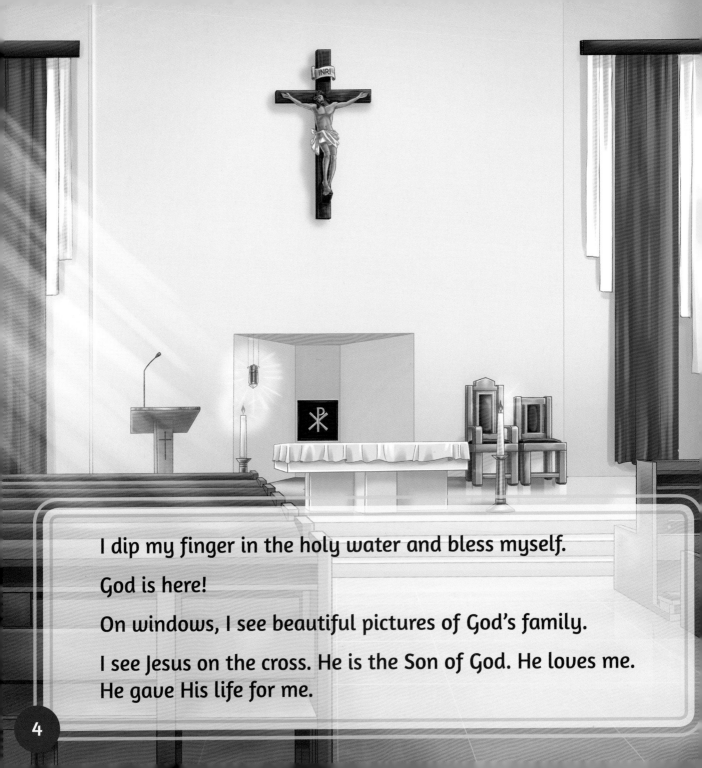

I dip my finger in the holy water and bless myself.

God is here!

On windows, I see beautiful pictures of God's family.

I see Jesus on the cross. He is the Son of God. He loves me. He gave His life for me.

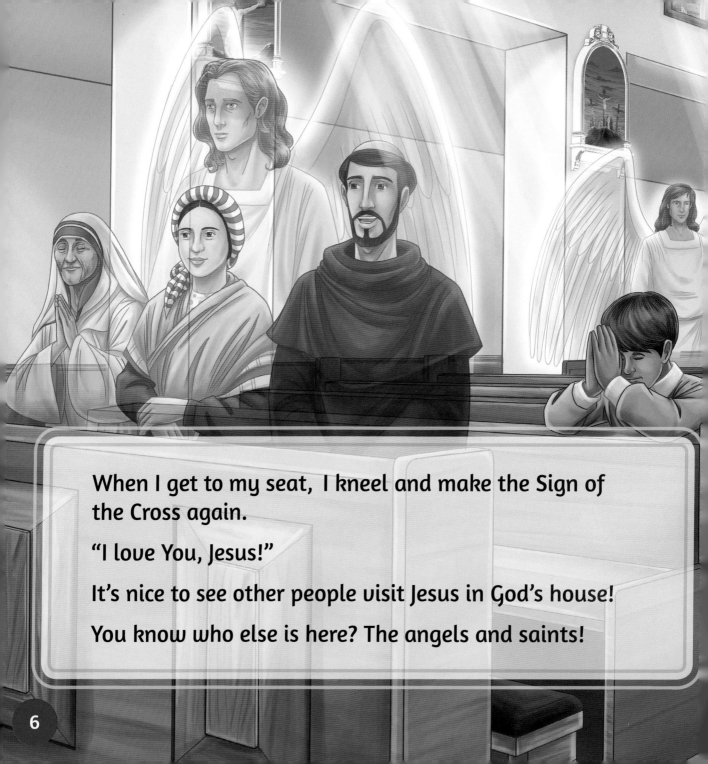

When I get to my seat, I kneel and make the Sign of the Cross again.

"I love You, Jesus!"

It's nice to see other people visit Jesus in God's house!

You know who else is here? The angels and saints!

I hear music! Someone is coming. I stand and look. It's the Priest and his helpers. Someone carries a beautiful book. It is the Word of God.

The Priest and his helpers go to the altar. Once there, the Priest and the Deacon kiss the altar.

This is the entrance procession!

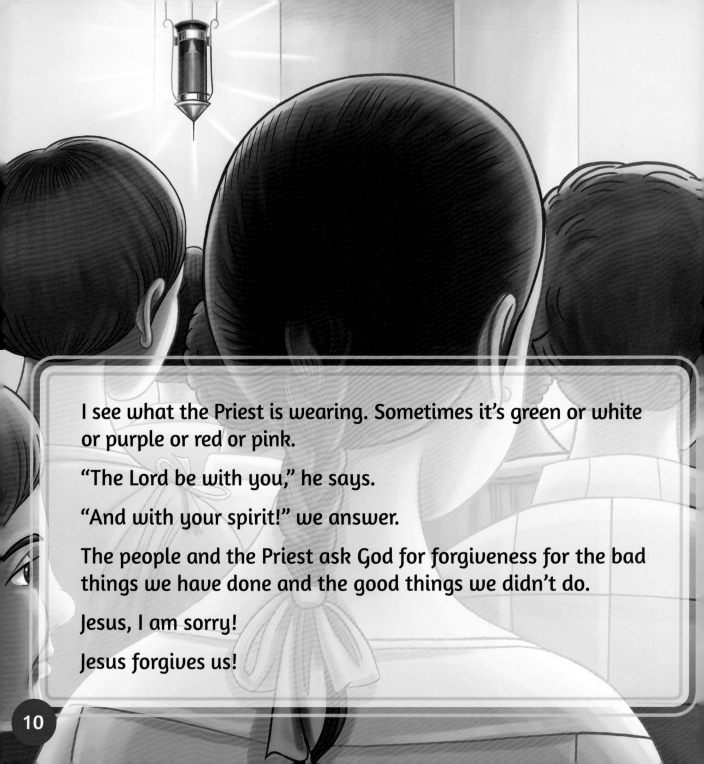

I see what the Priest is wearing. Sometimes it's green or white or purple or red or pink.

"The Lord be with you," he says.

"And with your spirit!" we answer.

The people and the Priest ask God for forgiveness for the bad things we have done and the good things we didn't do.

Jesus, I am sorry!

Jesus forgives us!

Someone is singing, and I sing, too!

We sing "Gloria" just like the angels did when Jesus was born!

We are so happy that God loves us and sent His Son!

The reader goes to the ambo and we sit down to hear the Word of God.

I hear how God did many things to help His people.

I learn how God can help me!

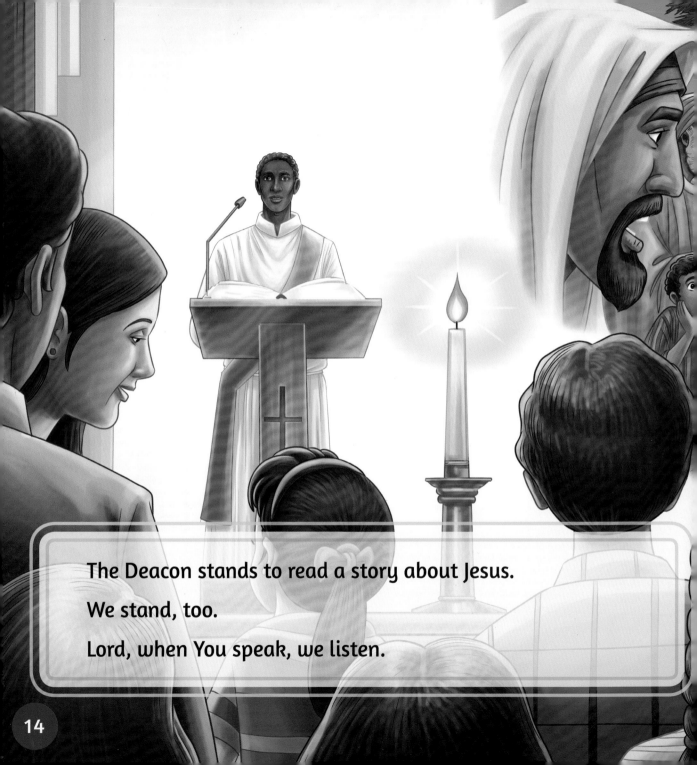

The Deacon stands to read a story about Jesus.

We stand, too.

Lord, when You speak, we listen.

Now the Priest speaks to us. He is like a shepherd guiding sheep. He tells us good things to help us every day!

The Priest follows in the footsteps of Jesus.

I believe in God.

I stand with my Church family, and we say aloud what we believe.

God tells us to pray for each other, and so we do.

"Lord, hear our prayer!"

God also wants us to help each other. We give to the church so the church can help others.

I like to place the envelope in the basket!

19

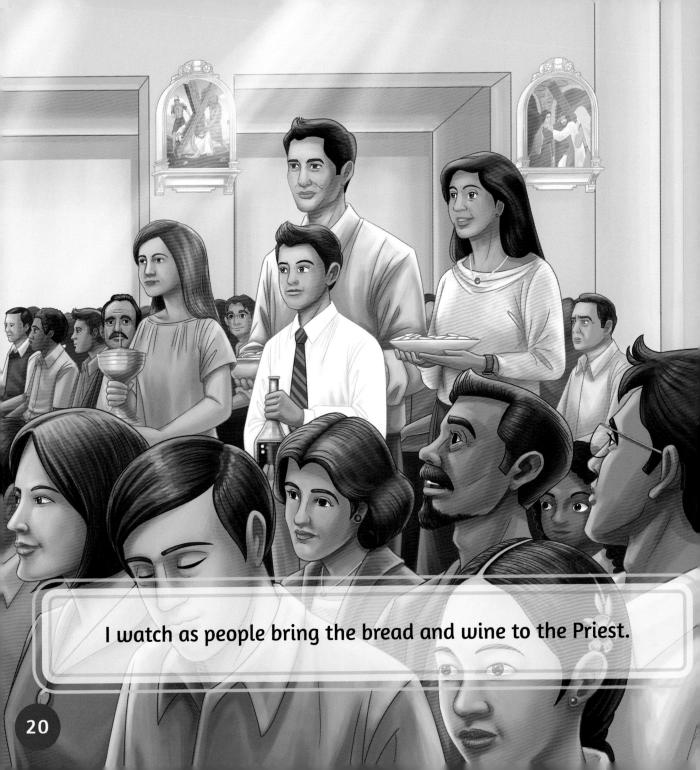

I watch as people bring the bread and wine to the Priest.

The Priest prepares the bread and wine which will become the Body and Blood of Christ.

We kneel. The Priest prays over the bread. The bread is now the Body of Christ.

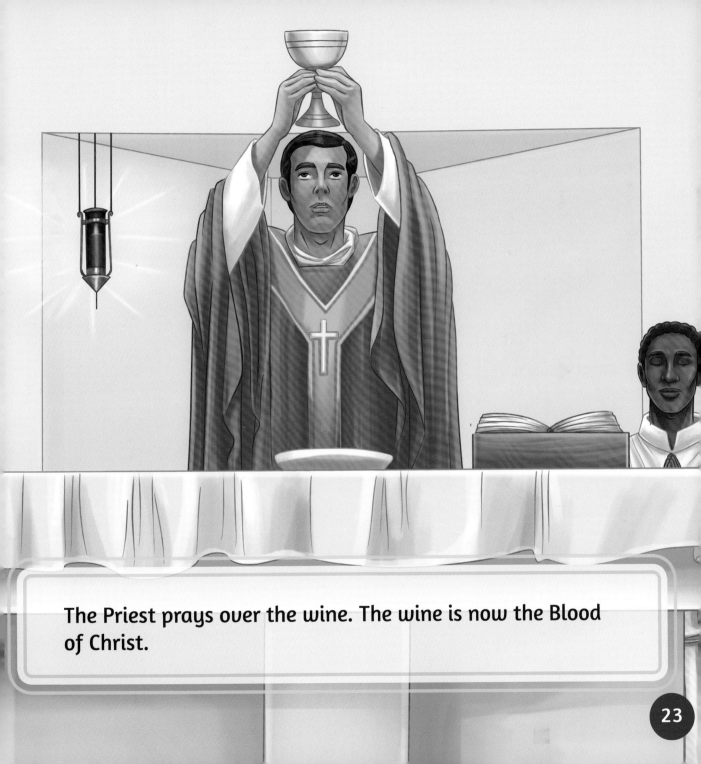

The Priest prays over the wine. The wine is now the Blood of Christ.

I stand to pray a special prayer with everybody.

"Our Father, Who art in heaven..." Jesus taught us that prayer.

"Peace be with you!" we say to each other. "Peace be with you!" they say back to us.

God wants us to be kind to each other. He wants us to get along.

We go to receive Jesus. Some people bow and receive the host and wine, now the Body and Blood of Jesus. Others cross their arms and receive a blessing.

Then we go to our seats and pray quietly.

"Thank You for Your love, Jesus! Thank You for giving Your life for me."

27

I see the Priest and the Deacon put everything away. Then the Priest blesses all of us and the Deacon says, "Go in peace. The Mass is ended."

We wait for the Priest and his helpers to leave. Then we leave, too.

I am leaving God's house, but He is with me.

What a happy thought!

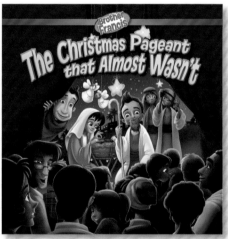

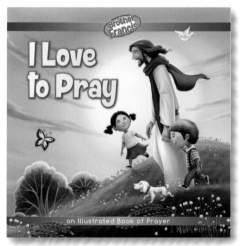

For more books like this one, visit:

www.brotherfrancisonline.com